I LOVE YOU M♥M

An Hachette UK Company
www.hachette.co.uk

First published in Great Britain in 2019 by Ilex, an imprint of
Octopus Publishing Group Ltd
Carmelite House
50 Victoria Embankment
London EC4Y 0DZ
www.octopusbooks.co.uk

Publisher: Alison Starling
Editorial Director: Helen Rochester
Commissioning Editor: Zara Anvari
Managing Editor: Frank Gallaugher
Editor: Jenny Dye
Assistant Editor: Stephanie Hetherington
Art Director: Ben Gardiner
Designer: Louise Evans
Assistant Production Manager: Lucy Carter

ISBN 978-1-78157-679-3

A CIP catalogue record for this book is available from the British Library.

Printed and bound in China

10 9 8 7 6 5 4 3 2 1

I LOVE YOU M♥M

LIZ TEMPERLEY

ilex

INTRODUCTION

There's nowhere warmer or safer than the embrace of a loving mother, and it is often only when we are older that we can fully appreciate the love and care we received as infants.

Put simply, mums are the best: they're always there to give us a tasty treat, bandage a grazed knee, listen to all our stories and comfort us when things go wrong. Where would we be without a mother's love?

This book highlights the many mums of the natural world who are devoted to their little ones. Some travel great distances to find the perfect food for a growing chick; some teach the vital skills a babe will need to grow into a successful adult, while others stop at nothing to defend their precious young from all possible dangers.

Motherhood is the most demanding and rewarding of roles, as these loving animals demonstrate. Let's go on a journey to meet nature's very best mums, and celebrate everything that makes our own mothers so special.

BOTTLENOSE DOLPHIN

Mums form a close and loving bond with their
little ones long before birth by talking and singing
to their growing bumps, and dolphins do exactly
the same thing. A mother dolphin will sing her
unique whistle again and again in the last two
weeks of pregnancy, helping the new baby to
recognise their mum's call and build a strong
relationship with her after being born.

AFRICAN ELEPHANT

Nine months may seem a long time, but just
imagine being pregnant for almost two years!
After a pregnancy lasting 22 months, an elephant
mother must be overjoyed to meet her new baby.
They will stay together for around 16 years, while
the mother teaches her little one everything
it needs to know about life.

BALD EAGLE

When you're in a safe, warm nest, with loving
parents bringing you all your food, it's hard to
imagine why you would ever want to leave. A bald
eagle mum will encourage her reluctant chicks to
practise jumping and flapping to nearby perches,
because she knows they'll need to spread
their wings and fly away one day.

EUROPEAN BADGER

We all want to give our babies the best home
possible, and badgers do this by digging out a
comfortable sett and lining it with a soft bedding
of bracken, moss and leaves. Badger mums
and dads clear out and replace old bedding
regularly, knowing that a clean home
is the best place for a young family.

JAPANESE RED BUG

Coping with a fussy eater isn't easy, but love keeps us searching for pleasing morsels for our little ones. Baby Japanese red bugs will eat only the sweetest, ripest fruits of one very rare type of tree, and their mothers willingly spend hours every day catering to their demanding tastes until they can take over the job themselves.

COMMON CHIMPANZEE

It's not just at school that we learn the skills
we need for life, but also in the arms of our loving
mothers. Female chimpanzees have been recorded
showing their young how to use tools to 'fish'
for tasty termites, and helping them when
they struggle. Thanks, Mum!

SOUTHERN AFRICAN MEERKAT

Raising a family is much easier when you have
plenty of help with babysitting. In a meerkat mob,
one dominant couple produce all the babies, but
the other members of the group are responsible
for protecting and feeding them. By working
together, they ensure the next generation
will grow and thrive.

THOMSON'S GAZELLE

We all have moments when we want to walk away from our children, especially at the height of a tantrum, but mamma gazelles have another reason for doing this. If they sense a potential threat to their babies, they will turn their backs on them and wander away in an attempt to draw the predator's attention towards themselves and away from their young.

POLAR BEAR

Being a mum is incredibly demanding.
A female polar bear prepares for impending
motherhood by doubling her body weight before
burying herself in a den of snow to give birth.
After her cubs are born, she stays underground
without eating for another two months until
her babies are strong enough to venture
into the world outside.

LARGE WHITE PIG

Pigs are famous for their intelligence and they
should be as widely praised for their mothering
skills. When they are able to spend their whole
lives together, a mother pig will care for her
babies by snuggling and grooming them even
after they have matured into adulthood.

LAYSAN ALBATROSS

Mothers are a dedicated bunch – and some
keep reproducing for years. Wisdom, a Laysan
albatross, has raised over 30 baby chicks,
returning each season to breed on Midway
Atoll in the Pacific. Still producing chicks
at 67, she's the best mother a baby
could ask for.

EASTERN GRAY KANGAROO

Nowhere feels safer than being with Mum,
and for a baby kangaroo, the safest place of all
is inside its mother's pouch. After six months
inside, suckling and growing, the baby joey is
ready to find out what's happening in the outside
world, but for another six weeks or so, home
is still where Mum is.

SOUTH AFRICAN CHEETAH

Spending time with babies brings out our playful side, and this is just as true for animals as it is for us. A cheetah mum will play with her cubs throughout the first year of life to establish a trusting bond and teach hunting skills that will be vital for her young when they grow up.

BROWN HARE

Baby hares are born ready to explore their
new worlds independently, but their mother
visits them every evening to give them milk until
they're ready to live on solid food. Each time they
part, the mother is careful to leap away so she
doesn't leave a scent trail: she wants her
babies to stay safe at all costs.

GRIZZLY BEAR

There's a reason we call an impressive mum
a mamma bear: a female grizzly bear will challenge
any other animal that poses a threat to her cubs,
even a hungry male bear. As well as feeding and
teaching her little ones, she never stops
looking out for their safety.

CANADA GOOSE

If we see our loved ones in danger, we all
discover our inner tiger – or should that be our
inner goose? When a Canada goose fears her
babies are being threatened, she will hiss at and
chase the potential attacker, even if they are much
larger than her. Parenthood makes us brave.

COMMON HIPPOPOTAMUS

Water helps to support and relax pregnant mothers, and for hippos, it's the perfect place to give birth. The new baby hippo swims to the surface to take its first breath and will spend much of its infant life swimming with its mother, even riding on her back when the water is too deep.

H O N E Y B E E

There are many different ways to build a family,
and for honey bees, families revolve around the
queen bee. The female workers collaborate to
protect the queen and attend to her every
need so she can focus on laying eggs.

GRAY LANGUR

As we grow old enough to start finding out about
the world around us, we open ourselves up to new
role models. In the same way, when a gray langur
baby reaches the age of two, its mum will allow
other females in the group to share mothering
duties, helping it to bond with its community.

AMERICAN QUARTER HORSE

Evidence suggests that a mother horse feels
love for her new foal: she is highly protective
of her little one in the days after giving birth.
Through sniffs, licks, soft whinnying and, of
course, suckling, she establishes a deep and
trusting bond with her new arrival.

EMPEROR PENGUIN

Motherhood is an endurance test, and never more
so than for an emperor penguin mum. After laying
just one egg, she will leave it with her partner
while she embarks on an epic 80-kilometre
journey to find fish. When she returns, she will
regurgitate food for her newly hatched baby
and take over the caring duties.

WEST AFRICAN GIRAFFE

Every mum needs a bit of help from her friends, and giraffes are no exception. Mother giraffes in a herd come together to form a crèche, with one mum looking after several babies, freeing up the others so they can roam free, look for food or simply have a break for a little while.

PALE-THROATED THREE-TOED SLOTH

Finding a place to live is a challenge faced
by almost every young person as they enter
adulthood. Young pale-throated three-toed sloths
have it easier, however, as when the time is right
their mothers give them their childhood territory,
moving on themselves to set up a new
home of their own.

MOUNTAIN GORILLA

Weaning can be a tricky process for parents and children. In a gorilla family, the dominant male silverback will take pressure off Mum during this period by playing with their infant. His role as an attachment figure provides both distraction and fun for a fractious little one.

AFRICAN LION

Lioness mums happily provide milk for each
other's babies, and teach their young to hunt,
ensuring that the group will be well provided for.
Females usually stay in the same pride for their
whole lives, doing most of the hunting, and their
strong bonds are key to the group's success.

RING-TAILED LEMUR

Newborn ring-tailed lemurs cling closely to
their mothers, but as they grow bigger and more
confident, they bounce away to play with other
youngsters in the group, wrestling with and
chasing each other. But when the playing
is over, they hurry back to the safety
of their mothers' cuddles.

L L A M A

When llama mums give birth, they face danger
from both predators and jealous males. To protect
a mother when she is in labour, a group of females
form a ring around her, so her baby can be born in
safety. There is infinite strength in sisterhood.

SEA OTTER

As well as being adorable, a baby sea otter's
fluffiness plays a vital role in its safety. A mother
sea otter will blow air into her baby's soft, dense
fur, puffing it up like a natural life jacket, so that
her little one can float safely until it learns to
swim and dive just like she does.

BORNEAN ORANGUTAN

Life with a human teenager can be a mixed
bag, involving rows and sulking, but this is not
the case for orangutans. After living in the warmth
of her mother's love for up to ten years, a young
female orangutan will continue to visit her mum
until she starts her own family at the
age of around sixteen.

GIANT PANDA

'Come on, it's time for bed,' is a call heard
in every household, and not just from human
mums. A mother panda in Taipei Zoo was filmed
wearily following her bouncy baby round their
enclosure until she finally managed to persuade
the little one to rest. We all face
the same struggles!

STRAWBERRY POISON-DART FROG

There's no rest for a new mum. After her
babies hatch, a mother strawberry poison-dart
frog carries each one to a bromeliad plant where
they can grow in pools of water between the
plant's leaves. She feeds them regularly with her
own unfertilised eggs, which contain everything
her babies need to grow as strong as she is.

PYGMY GOAT

The bonds between a mother and her child last for life. Even when the children are fully grown, goats will snuggle together, wrapping their necks around each other, and they can recognise family members after years of separation.

SOUTHERN KOALA

Every mammal mother wants to give her baby
the very best food to help it grow, especially
during the critical period of moving from milk
to solid food. A female koala predigests tough
eucalyptus leaves for her little one as part
of the weaning process, which prepares
it to move on to its adult diet.

GELADA BABOON

Our mums keep us close before gradually
helping us to find our own way. In just the same
way, a newborn gelada baboon holds on tightly
to its mother's belly. After five weeks, the infant
will clamber onto her back, from where it
can have a better view of the independent
life that's awaiting it.

HEREFORD COW

Cows demonstrate motherly love that lasts a lifetime. When they are allowed to grow old together, cows will nurse and groom their calves into adulthood. Fully grown calves will give their mothers just as much grooming as they receive, as their bond matures into one of true companionship.

NORTH AMERICAN RACOON

Even when we grow up, it's reassuring to
be close to our mums. After spending roughly
a year learning, playing and sleeping in the safety
of its mother's den, a young racoon often
chooses to establish its adult home
within easy reach of Mum.

NILE CROCODILE

Some of the fiercest people make the tenderest
of mothers. A crocodile mum watches over her
eggs for up to three months, protecting them from
predators. When the eggs hatch, she carries
her babies down to the water, holding
them delicately in her deadly jaws.

GRAY WOLF

Nothing is stronger than the bond between
a mother and her child, but other family
relationships are important too. Each wolf pack
is a haven of close and complex bonds between
siblings, cousins, aunts and uncles, and when the
alpha pair are in danger, all members of the family
will band together to protect them.

GREATER FLAMINGO

Flamingo mums benefit from having
very helpful partners. Instead of leaving
Mum to do all the work, the male flamingo
helps to build the nest and incubate the eggs,
and he even produces rich, nourishing milk
for their baby.

AMERICAN RED SQUIRREL

Life is easier when we look out for each other.
Red squirrels are fiercely territorial, but if a female
notices that a mother in a nearby territory has
become silent, she will investigate and adopt
any orphaned squirrel pups into her own family,
raising them as if they were her own.

GUINEA BABOON

Mothers are our first and most loving teachers,
always ready with a cuddle and a smile.
Young baboons practise their vital grooming
skills on their mothers and, even after they
have been weaned, often use this closeness
as a chance to slip in for some milk and
a brief return to babyhood.

BLACK RHINOCEROS

Single parenthood is a challenge, but it creates a
unique relationship with lots of joy. Each rhino
mum raises her baby by herself, and her love is
so strong that she won't mate again until her
little one becomes fully independent, a process
that can take two to three years.

SUFFOLK SHEEP

Children in search of adventure can easily
wander off, giving their parents a fright. A curious
lamb is likely to do just the same to its mother,
skipping away when her back is turned. Luckily,
they each know the other's unique call, and
Mum will bleat and search without rest
until they are reunited.

BENGAL TIGER

A mum's work is done when her baby is fully
independent and ready to face the world, but
there's no need to rush things. Even though
tiger cubs learn all the hunting skills they need
by the age of eighteen months, they stay with
their mothers until they are up to two
and a half years old.

ATLANTIC WALRUS

What's the best way to show our love for each
other? With a kiss, of course! Walrus mums adore
their babies just as much as we love ours, and as
well as snuggling them tightly in their flippers,
they give their little ones loving kisses to
show just how much they care.

ACKNOWLEDGEMENTS

I'd like to thank Zara, Jenny, Lucy and the rest
of the team at Octopus for the opportunity to
work on such a sweet, lovely book.

Big kisses to my family too.